UNDER MY GRANDMOTHER'S OLIVE TREE
And Other Poems About Being Palestinian

WASEEM NABULSI

ZA'ATAR PUBLISHING
H O U S E

Copyright © 2017 by Waseem Nabulsi

All rights reserved. This book or any portion thereof may not be reproduced or used in any manner whatsoever without the express written permission of the publisher except for the use of brief quotations in a book review.

Za'atar Publishing House

ZaatarPublishingHouse@gmail.com

First Printing, 2017

ISBN: 0-692-93455-3
ISBN-13: 978-0-692-93455-5

To my parents
and everybody who has
or continues to live under occupation.

CONTENTS

	Acknowledgments	i
1	Under My Grandmother's Olive Tree	1
2	Bullets and Stones	2
3	Lifta	4
4	Checkpoint Soldier	6
5	Here	8
6	Untitled No. 1	10
7	Indigenous	12
8	For My Grandfather	14
9	Checkpoint	16
10	Strangers	18
11	Old Friend	20
12	Israeli Privilege	22
13	2007	24
14	Routine	26
15	For My Mother	28
16	Gaza	30

ACKNOWLEDGMENTS

This book would not have been possible had it not been for the generosity and unwavering support of my parents and my sisters, Diana and Dalia. I would also be remiss if I did not acknowledge the essential help of my friend Riley Sanders in photographing my art—thank you so much Riley, you are truly a great friend. Finally, I wanted to thank all of my teachers—both at the St. Mark's School of Texas and at the Trinity School of Midland—for believing in me and believing in my abilities.

AUTHOR'S NOTE

I shall proclaim in my detention cell, in the bathroom, in the stable, under the lash, manacled, in the violence of chains, that a million birds on the branches of my heart, are singing fighting songs.
— MAHMOUD DARWISH, "Defiance"

When I began creating the following collection of poems and art, I did so without the intention of ever publishing it as it appears before you today. Rather, this book emerged as the byproduct of my own journey to more clearly define my sense of identity and how it relates to my Palestinian roots.

I began writing poetry sometime in middle school as a way to vent the frustration that I would feel after visiting Palestine during the summer. These poems, often written on the back side of old worksheets, usually ended up at the bottom of my dresser or hidden between books on my bookshelf. For a large portion of my developing years, poetry and art served as my diary in which I could confide my innermost thoughts, worries, and fears.

As I grew older, my poems and art transformed from one-dimensional verses depicting my own middle school angst, to poems that attempted to explore the dichotomy between the love of one's homeland and the pain of oppression. Using poetry and art, I set out to explore the uncomfortable and difficult topics that nobody wanted to talk about—topics like post-traumatic stress disorder, Israeli depopulation of Palestinian villages, and the bombings of Gaza, among many others.

My hope is that in reading this book, you, the reader, do not see it as exclusively representative of Palestinian identity; rather, my hope is that you see this collection of poetry and art as a broader reflection of the intricacies and struggles of the human condition.

UNDER MY GRANDMOTHER'S OLIVE TREE

Under My Grandmother's Olive Tree

Year after year, like a familiar acquaintance you've waited,
Between us an obvious familiarity, unstated.

As your branches grew longer and your trunk more gnarled,
My legs grew longer and my body grew stronger.

And each time we reunite, you kindly remind me that your fruit is not yet ripe,
But each and every time, I can't help but try,
Only to be prompted that its not yet your time.

So, I'll wait by your trunk, guarded by your shade,
Knowing that eventually a farewell must be bade.

But until then, under your shade, I'll tell you my stories,
Hoping one day to experience your glory.

Bullets and Stones

I've resigned myself to throwing stones
Because bullets and missiles have always meant the end,
And I'm tired of picking up the bones of my friends.

But, I've resigned myself to throwing stones
Because even though hope is dead,
My soul breathes alive and well.

So fire your lead,
Let it pierce my flesh;
Rip my wounds open afresh.

You can draw your weapons and fire your drones,
But you will never take my stones.

Waseem Nabulsi, *Bullets and Stones,* acrylic on fragment of Lifta house brick, 6 x 5.5 x 2.5 cm

Lifta

Scattered across the hilltop like jasmine on its vine,
They crumble solemnly, dignified.

Decaying not dead,
The walls contain hopes that no bulldozer could tear down,
And the stairs bear truthes the largest checkpoint could not keep out.
The bricks as well remain not as remnants of the past,
Rather as witnesses to atrocious acts.

These buildings stand not silent,
They scream defiantly,
Not abandoned, not ghost town;
They scream *war crime*.

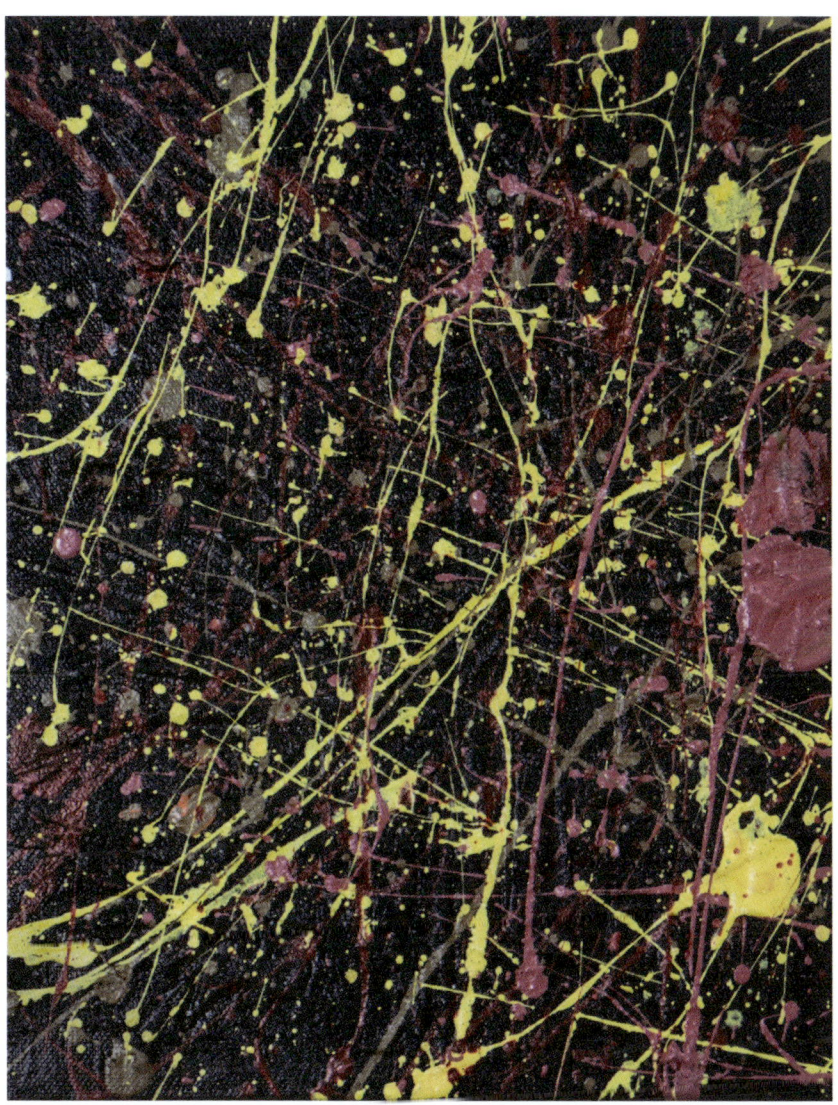

Waseem Nabulsi, *Seven Deadly Sins: Wrath,* acrylic on canvas, 25 x 20 cm

Checkpoint Soldier

It's a metal cage with soldiers waiting,
Gun slung across his chest, misguided hatred.
Red flashes of cars decelerating,
The value of humanity grows less and less sacred.

Gum and pillow venders line the street,
The soldier, indifferent, spits hatred like shots from his gun.
Images still fresh of the bullet hole riddled 15-year-old left out in the sun,
Dying to escape, but knowing that death is imminent if they run.

In the land of the checkpoint, death comes cheaper,
And soldiers stand waiting—assistants to the Grim Reaper.

But life goes on for the Palestinian people,
Because for seventy years they have fought against evil,
And for hundreds of more years they will fight for their freedom.

Waseem Nabulsi, *Resistance*, acrylic on canvas, 50.5 x 40 cm

Here

The bread tastes better here, he says.
The bread tastes better here and the jasmine smells stronger here.
Here, the fruit like the nighttime wind is sweeter.
And even the caged bird chirps louder here

Because here is where my roots run deep,
And here is where my forefathers sleep.
And even if they don't want me here,
I can never leave because here is where I'm meant to be.

Here, they try to fence us in,
But I, like the caged bird, am louder here
Because on this land,
Life feels better here.

UNDER MY GRANDMOTHER'S OLIVE TREE

Waseem Nabulsi, *Keffiyeh Fingerprint,* acrylic on wood, 30.1 x 18.3 cm

Untitled No. 1

They say that when you die your soul leaves your body to watch one last time,
But today my soul died and as my body left my soul,
I stood by and watched motionless.

Because my body left my soul long ago when you pointed your gun at my head and didn't shoot,
Because sometimes I wish you would have shot when your gun was pointed at my head,
So that I wouldn't have to relive my death over and over again.

And today my body left my soul when I saw you bruise her ankle and heard her cry out in pain,
Because up until then she had been my comfort from pain,
And you took the only thing keeping me sane.

And part of my soul died when I realized that pure evil is real,
Because, with a gun, it stood in my presence,
Drenched in the blood of my childhood innocence.

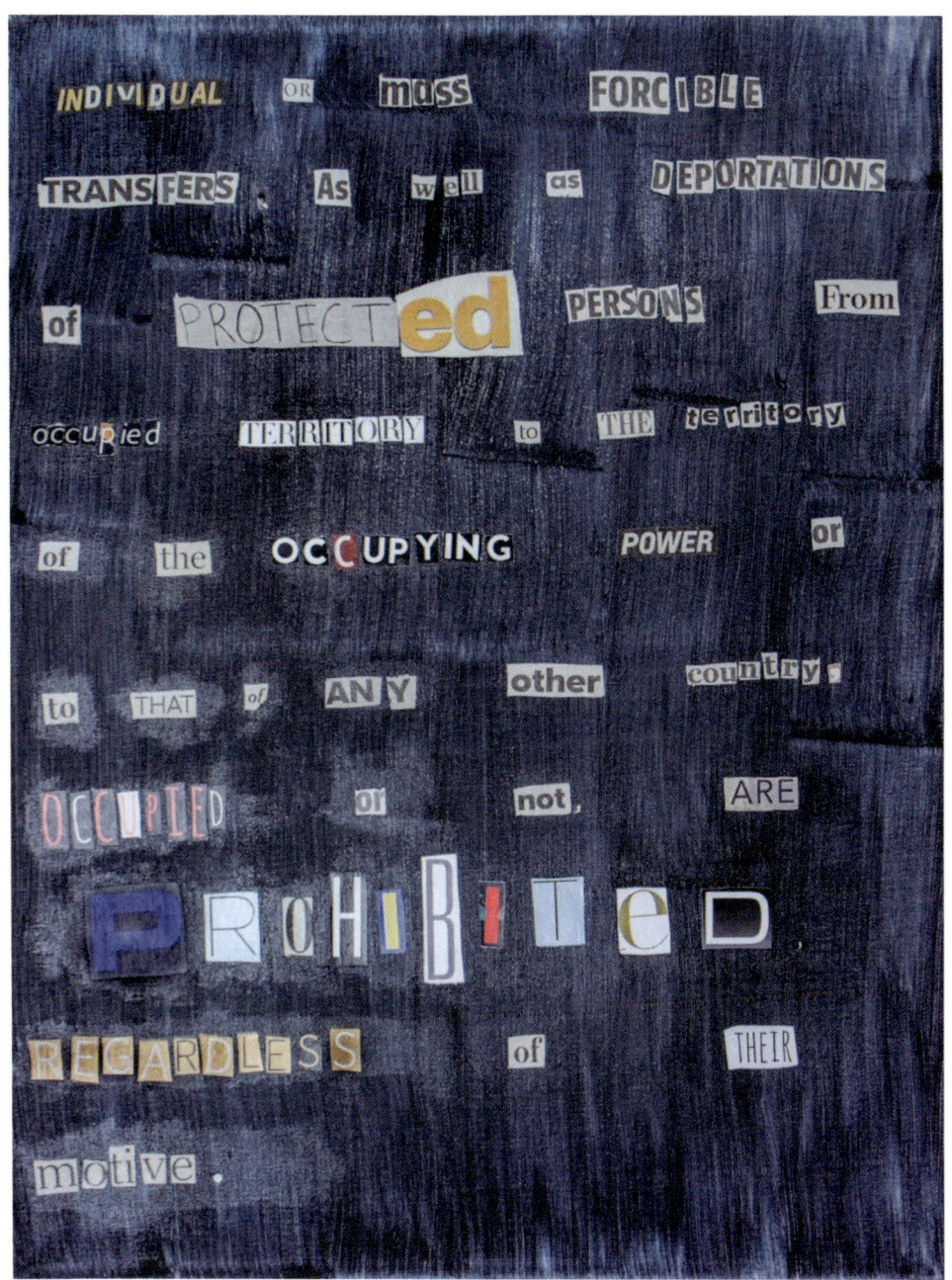

Waseem Nabulsi, *Geneva Convention: Article 49*, mixed media on canvas, 60.5 x 45 cm

Indigenous

If my land could talk,
Could I use it as witness?

Would the world believe me if the
trees, in all their wisdom, testified to
the crimes—crimes with victims?

If the soil, rich with my ancestors,
could speak,
Would anyone listen?

If my land could weep,
Then would someone help us?

Waseem Nabulsi, *The Nakba,* watercolor on paper, 30.5 x 22.5 cm

For My Grandfather

Time has been cruel to him;
No mercy, it makes a fool of him.
He curses his father
While time, like a curtain, blindfolds him.

He purses his lips not because he's mad,
But because time has gone by too fast,
And he can't remember the past.

Eyes glossy, eyebrows scrunched,
Over a tissue box, he stands hunched.

He is lost,
But this time he can't be found.
Clutching the remaining shards of his youth,
His tears fall without a sound.

He's lost his way,
He's not fine,
Speak to me, Father Palestine.

Waseem Nabulsi, *Old City*, 2017, photograph of a street in the Old City of Nablus

Checkpoint

The day I faced the barrel,
My faith was shattered.

That day I faced the barrel,
I screamed and resisted because at that moment, nothing mattered.

I clutched my life and begged it not to leave me,
But the ground beneath me began to falter,
And my knees deceived me.

But it wasn't my time,
So I dusted myself off,
I wiped my face and held my tears back with a cough.

My shoes were dusty and my ankles bruised,
But my determination didn't falter;
I refused.

But even till now the image still haunts me,
Damn you Soldier,
Your barrel has <u>never</u> left me.

Waseem Nabulsi, *Micro-Aggressions,* acrylic on canvas, 7.5 x 7.5 cm

Strangers

Siti, there are strangers in our house.

They have taken the room where my father was birthed and the kitchen where he was first nursed.
The women even wears your blouse--she says it's now hers.

Siti, there are strangers in our house,
And despite my loudest screams and shouts,
They won't get out.

Siti, there are strangers in our house,
And I need to go back
Because I've begun to forget the scent of the jasmine that sprouts just outside of the house.

Siti, there are strangers in our house,
And they won't leave because they claim it has always been theirs,
But the deed,
The deed says it's ours.

Waseem Nabulsi, *The Key to Return,* papier-mâché sculpture overlaid on 19th century maps of Palestine, 72 x 55 cm

Old Friend

Speak to me oh sea of mine,
    Be kind to me,
    Make up for lost time.

Feed me oh sea of mine,
    Nourish my soul,
    Fill my mind.

Sing to me oh sea of mine,
    Remind me of your ageless hymn,
    Fill my ears with your careless rhyme.

Be with me oh sea of mine,
    It has been decades since you've truly been mine.

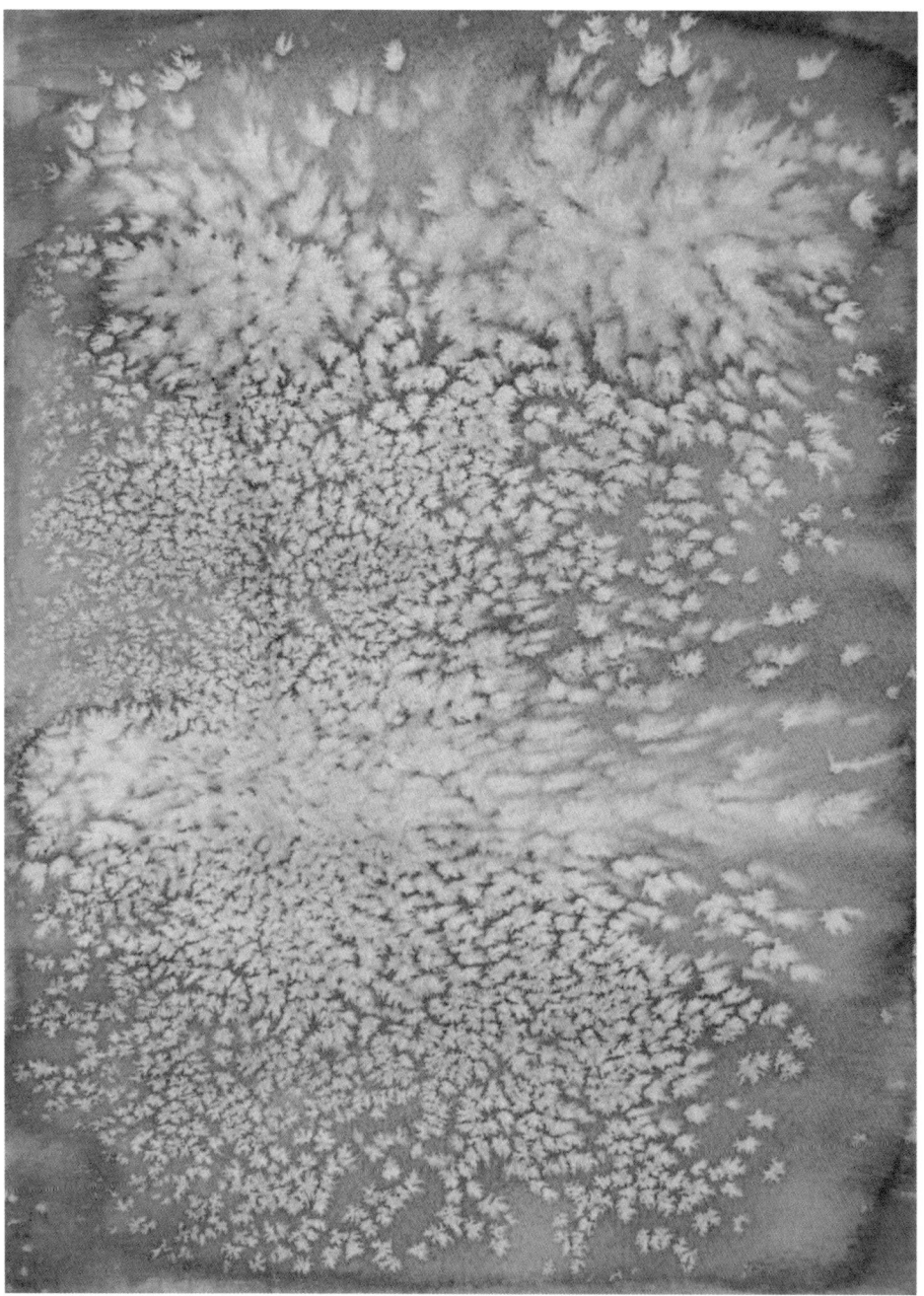

Waseem Nabulsi, *Haifa Sea,* watercolor on paper, 30.5 x 22.5 cm

Israeli Privilege

I can't imagine how you can sleep well,
While we are here in a living hell.

While you sip your wine and eat enough for an entire family each,
I hope you remember young Mohamed, Zakaria, Ahmed, and Ismail, who were murdered while playing on the Gazan beach.

While you swim in your pools and water your flowers,
I hope you think of the Palestinian mothers shot dead from watch towers.

And when you serve in the army and wave your gun in my face,
I just hope you'll be able to forget what you did,
Because that is an image I have never been able to erase.

Waseem Nabulsi, *Seven Deadly Sins: Greed,* mixed media acrylic on canvas, 25 x 20 cm

2007

Wedged between a cane and a lit cigarette,
I closed my eyes for a minute.
Degraded and disregarded,
My sense of surrender beckoned.

I stood in a cage, no longer human,
Rather, I stood there as another piece of a cruel
game of Tetris.

With the pain of experience on my left and the
pain of optimism on my right,
I had a clear choice to make:
Resign to my fate or hope for the future.
Alone with my thoughts,
I decided on neither.

I will not be the dreamer,
I am a believer.
I love this land,
And for that I'll never leave her

They say to look forward and never look back,
But the only way to solve this conflict is revisiting
the past.

So I will fight and struggle till the final stone is cast,
Only stopping when there is justice at last.

Waseem Nabulsi, *Checkpoint,* 2017, photograph of the now-abandoned Huwwara Checkpoint outside the West Bank city of Nablus.

Routine

Usual Jerusalem heat,
Back of the bus seat,
Go to sleep, wake up—repeat.

Trying not to think about my tired feet,
I walk down the dimly lit street.

Armed soldiers stare at me,
I stare back not scared, but defiantly,
Knowing I have miles to go before I can sleep.

Waseem Nabulsi, *Jerusalem Streets,* 2017, photograph of a street in the Armenian Quarter of the Old City of Jerusalem

For my Mother

Distracted, she stands,
She feels out of place.
Anxious, she fidgets,
A pain on her face.

She looks in the distance,
Searching for strength,
The sound of gunshots;
She tries not to break.

The smell of teargas,
A familiar scent,
Brings her back to her childhood,
And the blood she saw spent.

And even till now,
Though her past still does haunt her,
She cannot give up,
She will not surrender,
She must keep fighting,
For the land that bore her.

Waseem Nabulsi, ***Dusk at Jericho,*** 2017, photograph of the Jericho landscape at sunset

Gaza

She counts herself lucky, she says.

She counts herself lucky that when bombs fell from the sky,
Neither her parents nor her siblings died.

She counts herself lucky that when her school was flattened down,
Her parents had the money to send her out of town.

She says she is lucky that after thousands of bombs,
Her family still has a roof over their heads, a place to call home.

She calls herself lucky because even though they won't let her return,
She still keeps the memories of the place she was born.

And when I ask her where she'd rather be,
Her lips utter the word: *Falastine*.

Waseem Nabulsi, *Palestinian Nights,* 2017, photograph of the Palestinian village of Majd Al-Krum

WASEEM NABULSI was born and raised in Texas by two Palestinian immigrant parents. He is currently a high school senior at an all-boys school in Dallas.

To inquire about the purchase of any of the art featured in this book, please send an email to ZaatarPublishingHouse@gmail.com.

Printed in Poland
by Amazon Fulfillment
Poland Sp. z o.o., Wrocław